D0777331

To Beth,

Love
Janet

Morning Coffee and Time Alone

BRIGHT PROMISE FOR A NEW DAY

Compiled by ALICE GRAY

Art by SUSAN MINK COLCLOUGH

BLUE COTTAGE GIFTS™
a Division of Multnomah Publishers, Inc.
Sisters, Oregon

Morning Coffee and Time Alone
© 2001 by Blue Cottage Gifts™
Published by Blue Cottage Gifts™, a division of Multnomah Publishers, Inc.®
P.O. Box 1720, Sisters, OR 97759

ISBN 1-58860-007-6

Artwork by Susan Mink Colclough
Artwork designs by Susan are reproduced under license from ©Arts Uniq',
Inc.®, Cookeville, TN and may not be reproduced without permission.
For information regarding art prints featured in this book, please contact:
Arts Uniq'
P.O. Box 3085
Cookeville, TN 38502
1-800-223-5020

Designed by Koechel Peterson & Associates, Minneapolis, Minnesota

Multnomah Publishers, Inc. has made every effort to trace the ownership of
all poems and quotes. In the event of a question arising from the use of a poem
or quote, we regret any error made and will be pleased to make the necessary
correction in future editions of this book.

Please see the acknowledgments at the back of the book for complete attributions
for this material.

Scripture quotations are taken from The Holy Bible,
New International Version (NIV)
© 1973, 1984 by International Bible Society,
used by permission of Zondervan Publishing House,
and New American Standard Bible (NASB) © 1960, 1977, 1995
by the Lockman Foundation. Used by permission.

Printed in China

01 02 03 04 05 06—10 9 8 7 6 5 4 3 2 1 0

www.gift-talk.com

Contents

Morning Coffee and Time Alone

Today is a GIFT, wrapped in gold, ribboned with promise, and delivered to our door before sunrise. Why shouldn't we take time to open the package slowly, pondering its contents?

With coffee in hand, I awake with pleasure to this brief, blessed interval of peace when I am alone with my thoughts. This is the time to remember, to reflect…and to dream. The cup in my hand brings its blessing of warmth and savory aroma.

A new day of life, after all, is no small treasure. It ought to be welcomed with peace and hope. Curling up into some cozy corner on the sunrise side of the house, we take time to collect our thoughts and to consider the day that lies ahead.

The stories you hold in your hand remind us that each day of life—in fact, each moment—is precious. So pour yourself a fresh cup of coffee, friend, and watch the rising sun chase away the shadows.

Now Playing...

ANN CAMPSURE

Celestial nightlights adorn
the open theatre of predawn sky;
the moon rolls out its golden carpet
across the placid lake below.
The lights dim—
wind holds its breath
as the velvet curtain of night
begins its slow ascent.
From eastern wings, pale streaks of dawn
give hue and shape to the set;
thin shadows frame silhouettes
of characters and scenery.

The hush deepens…

finally broken by the first trills

of one lone robin warming up for the overture.

The stage is set;

the cast awaits its cue—

the author nods and smiles,

then bids the day begin.

Hope is a good breakfast.

FRANCES BACON

The Trouble Tree

A UTHOR   UNKNOWN

The carpenter I hired to help me restore an old farmhouse had just finished a rough first day on the job. A flat tire made him lose an hour of work, his electric saw quit, and now his ancient pickup truck refused to start.

While I drove him home, he sat in stony silence. On arriving, he invited me in to meet his family. As we walked toward the front door, he paused briefly at a small tree, touching the tips of the branches with both hands. When opening the door, he underwent an amazing transformation. His tanned face was wreathed in smiles and he hugged his two small children and gave his wife a kiss.

Afterward he walked me to the car. We passed the tree and my curiosity got the better of me. I asked him about what I had seen him do earlier. "Oh, that's my trouble

Enjoy the blessings of the day if God sends them, and the evils bear patiently and sweetly; for this day only is ours.

JEREMY TAYLOR

tree," he replied. "I know I can't help having troubles on the job, but one thing's for sure. Troubles don't belong in the house with my wife and children. So I just hang them up on the tree every night when I come home. Then in the morning I pick them up again.

"Funny thing is," he said with a smile, "when I come out in the morning to pick 'em up, there ain't nearly as many as I remember hanging up the night before."

I have had many troubles in my life, but the worst of them never came.

JAMES A. GARFIELD

A Fresh Perspective

BARBARA JOHNSON

The day started out rotten. I overslept and was late for work. Everything that happened at the office contributed to my nervous frenzy. By the time I reached the bus stop for my homeward trip, my stomach was one big knot.

As usual, the bus was late—and jammed. I had to stand in the aisle. As the lurching vehicle pulled me in all directions, my gloom deepened.

Then I heard a deep voice from up front boom, "Beautiful day, isn't it?" Because of the crowd, I could not see the man, but I could hear him as he continued to comment on the spring scenery, calling attention to each approaching landmark. This church. That park. This cemetery. That firehouse. Soon all the passengers were gazing out the windows. The man's enthusiasm was so contagious I found myself smiling for the first time that day. We reached my stop. Maneuvering toward the door, I got a look at our "guide": a plump figure with a black beard, wearing dark glasses, and carrying a thin white cane.

No one has any right to go about unhappy. He owes it to himself, to his friends, to society, and to the community in general, to live up to his best spiritual possibilities, not only now and then...but every day and every hour.

LILIAN WHITING

Yesterday and Tomorrow

ROBERT J. BURDETTE

There are two days in every week about which we should not worry—two days that should be kept free from any fear and apprehension. One of these days is Yesterday, with its mistakes and cares, its aches and pains, its faults and blunders. Yesterday has passed forever beyond our control. All the money in the world cannot bring back Yesterday. We cannot undo a single act we performed; we cannot erase a single word we said; we cannot rectify a single mistake. Yesterday has passed forever beyond recall. Let it go.

The other day we should not worry about is Tomorrow, with its possible adversities, its burdens, its large promise, and poor performance. Tomorrow also is beyond our immediate control. Tomorrow's sun will rise either in splendor or behind a mass of clouds—but it will rise. And until it does, we have no stake in Tomorrow, because it is as yet unborn.

That leaves us but one day—Today! And a person can fight the battles of just one day.

Yesterday and Tomorrow are futile worries. Let us, therefore, resolve to journey no more than one day at a time.

Therefore do not worry about tomorrow, for tomorrow will worry about itself. Each day has enough trouble of its own.

MATTHEW 6:34, NIV

Tomorrow you have no business with.
You steal if you touch tomorrow. It is God's.
Every day has in it enough to keep any
man occupied without concerning
himself with the things beyond.

HENRY WARD BEECHER

The Storekeeper

AUTHOR UNKNOWN

from Ladies Home Journal magazine

"How's business, Eben?"

The old man was washing at the sink after his day's work.

"Fine, Marthy, fine."

"Does the store look just the same? Land, how I'd like to be there again with the sun shining in so bright! How does it look, Eben?"

"The store's never been the same since you left it, Marthy." A faint flush came into Martha's cheeks. Is a wife ever too old to be moved by her husband's praise!

> *Love is that condition in which the happiness of another person is essential to your own.*
>
> ROBERT A. HEINLEIN

For years Eben and Martha had kept a tiny notion store, but one day Martha fell sick and was taken to the hospital. That was months ago. She was out now, but she would never be strong again—never more be partner in the happy little store.

"I can't help hankering for a sight of the store," thought Martha one afternoon. "If I take it real careful I think I can get down there. 'Tisn't so far."

It took a long time for her to drag herself downtown, but at last she stood at the head of the little street where the store was. All of a sudden she stopped. Not far from her on the pavement stood Eben. A tray hung from his neck. On this tray were arranged a few cards of collar buttons, some papers of pins and several bundles of shoe-laces. In a trembling voice he called his wares.

Martha leaned for support against the wall of a building nearby. She looked over the way at the little store. Its windows were filled with fruit. Then she understood. The store had gone to pay her hospital expenses. She turned and hurried away as fast as her weak limbs would carry her.

"It will hurt him so to have me find it out!" she thought, and the tears trickled down her face.

"He's kept it a secret from me, and now I'll keep it a secret from him. He shan't ever know that I know."

That night when Eben came in, chilled and weary, Martha asked cheerily the old question:

"How's business, Eben?"

"Better 'n ever, Marthy," was the cheery answer, and Martha prayed God might bless him for his sunshiny spirit and love of her.

The Red Umbrella

Retold by TANIA GRAY

As the drought continued for what seemed an eternity, a small community of Midwest farmers were in a quandary as to what to do. The rain was important not only in order to keep the crops healthy, but to sustain the townspeople's very way of living. As the problem became more urgent, the local church felt it was time to get involved and planned a prayer meeting in order to ask for rain.

In what seemed a vague remembrance of an old Native American ritual, the people began to show. The pastor soon arrived and watched as his congregation continued to file in. He slowly circulated from group to group as he made his way to the front in order to officially begin the meeting. Everyone he encountered was visiting across the aisles, enjoying the chance to socialize with their close friends. As the pastor finally secured his place in front of his flock, his thoughts were on the importance of quieting the crowd and starting the meeting.

Just as he began asking for quiet, he noticed an eleven-year-old girl sitting in the front row. She was angelically beaming with excitement and lying next to her was her bright red umbrella, poised for use. The beauty and innocence of this sight made the pastor smile to himself as he realized the faith this young girl possessed that the rest of the people in the room seemed to have forgotten. For the rest had come just to pray for rain…she had come to see God answer.

———— 🍃 ————

Now faith is the assurance of things hoped for, the conviction of things not seen.

HEBREWS 11:1, NAS

Morning Song

RUTH BELL GRAHAM
from Legacy of a Pack Rat

I had been getting up early, fixing myself a cup of coffee, and then sitting in the rocker on the front porch while I prayed for each of our children, and for each of theirs.

One morning I awoke earlier than usual. It was five o'clock, with dawn just breaking over the mountains.

Suddenly, I realized a symphony of bird song was literally surrounding me. The air was liquid with music, as if the whole creation were praising God at the beginning of a new day. I chuckled to hear the old turkey gobbler that had recently joined our family, gobbling away down in the woods at the top of his voice as if he were a song sparrow!

And I learned a lesson. I had been beginning my days with petitions, and I should have been beginning them with praise.

─────── ❦ ───────

Be true to your time in the morning.

CHARLES DICKENS

*He who every morning plans
the transactions of the day and
follows out that plan carries a thread
that will guide him through the
labyrinth of the most busy life.*

VICTOR HUGO

The Beautiful Wife

CARLA MUIR

A young girl was sitting with her friend at church on a bright Sunday morning. After preaching a sermon on having a grateful heart, the pastor asked if people would come forward and share something for which they were thankful. The visiting girl listened intently as people rattled off their blessings. A distinguished man in his late fifties was the last to speak. He bragged on and on about his "beautiful wife." He spoke of her encouraging words, and strong faith in the Lord. He closed by thanking his wife for marrying him thirty-two years ago. There was a roar of amens as the congregation agreed that he was indeed fortunate to have married her.

By now the young girl was looking around, trying to figure out who this beautiful, saintly woman was. Since the church was large, she finally gave up and asked her friend if she by chance knew who the wife was. "Oh yes," she replied, "everyone knows her. I'll point her out to you after church." After two more songs and a closing prayer, the service ended. As they slowly made their way up the

*I think true love is never blind
But rather brings an added light,
An inner vision quick to find
The beauties hid from common sight.*

PHOEBE CARY

aisle, her friend pointed and said, "She's over there in the corner." There an attractive woman was standing in a brilliant blue dress, laughing and chatting with a woman who had obviously been in a wheelchair for many years. The woman in the blue dress reached down and gave the smiling, frail woman a big hug.

"So that's the beautiful wife that man was talking about," observed the young visitor, looking at the woman in her brilliant blue dress.

"Yes, it is!" replied her friend, admiring the woman in the wheelchair.

*Your cheerful courage is a richer fortune
to you than money can ever be,
while your contented mind will brighten
life with truest happiness for one
who can find sunshine everywhere.*

LOUISA MAY ALCOTT

Under Construction

PHILIP GULLEY
from Front Porch Tales

My hobby is woodworking and has been for a number of years. My foray into wood began when we needed a kitchen table and my wife suggested I build one. We were low on money, and I was between college and graduate school and had the time. I'd never built anything before, but a kitchen table seemed as good a place to start as any.

My grandfather had a workshop set up in the family barn. I'd go there in the morning, turn on the heater, and walk around sniffing the workshop odors. Grandpa had lubricated the drill press once a month since 1950, and I could smell nearly forty years of oil buildup in the corner where it sat. Over by the table saw I smelled sawdust. After a while I became a sawdust connoisseur and could tell the difference between pine sawdust and cherry sawdust. There are few scents more pleasant. The dog slept in the workshop, and I could smell her, too, wet and stagnant, like the pond used to smell with its August coat of scum.

It took me the month of February to build the table. I could have done it quicker, but being tucked away in the barn while winter blasted away outside was so pleasant it made me want to dwell on that page as long as I could. In March, I took the table outside beneath the trees, next to the crocuses that were pushing up, and sanded it down. Grandpa came by and taught me how to use slivers of glass to plane the joints smooth. That's an old woodworker's trick I never would have picked up on my own.

I spent a week massaging five coats of tung oil into the wood. It takes a long time to get the finish right on a piece of furniture, but you can't hurry it, or the flaws will show, and all your hard work will be for nothing. Woodworking is a good way to learn that doing something worthwhile takes time. It is possible to make a table in a hurry. It is not possible, however, to make a table worth passing on to your grandchildren in a hurry.

My wife and I wrapped the table in blankets, loaded it up in the truck, and carried it home. She gave me a brass plate, engraved with my name and the year, to mount on its underbelly. That's so when my children's children play underneath it, they'll be able to see when Grandpa built it.

I wanted to buy chairs to match, but we didn't have the money so we made do. Though every time we'd go into an antique store, we'd keep our eyes peeled. I even thought about making chairs, but building a good chair is extraordinarily difficult and time-consuming. I could build a bad chair in a day. After six years of haunting antique stores, we found four chairs. By then, times were better, and we took them home. Each is as fine a chair as can be had, and I intend to enjoy myriad ears of July sweet corn while sitting in them.

A friend came for dinner not long ago. He asked me where I had bought my table, and I told him I had made it. He wanted me to make him one, but I told him no. A man has to be careful not to let his hobby become his business. He was talking about how his kitchen table is forever falling apart and lamenting the shoddy nature of today's craftsmanship. People slapping things together in five minutes expecting them to last a lifetime.

We got to talking about how that isn't only true about furniture, it's true about life. Folks get discouraged because God doesn't make them saints overnight. They don't understand all the years of God-work that go into making one's life a thing of beauty—a lot of shaping, a lot of smoothing, a lot of finishing. And if we rush the process, the flaws will surely show.

Once a week I rub a coat of lemon oil into my table. It reminds me that my table is never really finished. Kind of like me.

Accept life daily not as a cup to be drained but as a chalice to be filled with whatsoever things are honest, pure, lovely, and of good report.

SIDNEY LOVETT

Glory in the Morning

LINDA ANDERSEN
from Slices of Life

———❦———

It's 5:30 A.M., and Day knocks at the dark doors of
Night. I sit on my porch swing under a dark-green umbrella
of maple leaves that hover maternally over the porch roof.
And I wait for Sun.

A thin wisp of steam hovers expectantly over the coffee
cup I hold. The air vibrates with ecstatic birdsong. Cat
curls beside me for her final nap before breakfast. Morning
glories prepare to unfurl the blue trumpets. Then it happens,
and I am as awestruck as if I had never seen a sunrise.

Curtains of Night draw back silently, and Sun bursts
merrily over the blue haze of distant hills, painting earth

in green and brown stripes. It is morning…and it is glorious!

I listen, and hear Sun whistle a song of new opportunity. I hear Nature's first day-song waiting to be sung, and am reminded that "this is the day the Lord has made." And I decided to "rejoice and be glad in it."

Contentment Is...

RUTH SENTER

I heard the voice but couldn't see the person. She was on the other side of the locker, just coming in from her early morning swim. Her voice sounded like the morning itself—bright, cheerful, and full of life. At 6:15 in the morning, it would catch anyone's attention. I heard its affirming tone.

"Delores, I really appreciated the book you picked up for me last week. I know the library was out of your way. I haven't been able to put the book down. Solzhenitsyn is a great writer. I'm glad you suggested him to me."

"Good morning, Pat," she greeted another swimmer. For a moment the melodious voice was silent, then I heard it again. "Have you ever seen such a gorgeous day? I spied a pair of meadowlarks as I walked over this morning. Makes you glad you're alive, doesn't it?"

The voice was too good to be true. Who can be that

thankful at this time of the morning? Her voice had a note of refinement to it. Probably some rich woman who has nothing to do all day but sip tea on her verandah and read Solzhenitsyn. I suppose I could be cheerful at 6 A.M. if I could swim and read my way through the day. Probably even owns a cottage in the north woods.

I rounded the corner toward the showers and came face to face with the youthful voice. She was just packing her gear. Her yellow housekeeping uniform hung crisp and neat on her fiftyish frame. It was a uniform I'd seen before— along with mops, brooms, dust cloths, and buckets. An employee of the facility at which I swam. She flashed a smile my way, picked up her plastic K-Mart shopping bag,

A contented mind is the greatest blessing a man can enjoy in this world.

CHARLES DICKENS

*Very little is needed to make a
happy life. It is all within yourself,
in your way of thinking.*

MARCUS AURELIUS

and hurried out the door, spreading "have a glorious day" benedictions as she went.

I still had the yellow uniform on my mind as I swam my laps and sank down among the foamy lather of the whirlpool. My two companions were deep in conversation. At least one of them was. His tired, sad voice told tragic woes of arthritic knees, a heart aneurysm, sleepless nights, and pain-filled days.

Nothing was good or right. The water was too hot, the whirlpool jets weren't strong enough for his stiff knees, and his doctors had been much too slow in diagnosing his case. With his diamond-studded hand, he wiped the white suds out of his face. He looked ancient, but I suspected he too was fiftyish.

The yellow uniform and the diamond-studded ring

stood out in striking, silent contrast, proof to me again that when God says, "Godliness with contentment is great gain," He really means it. This morning I saw both contentment and discontent. I resolved never to forget.

Don't take things too seriously.
Live a life of serenity, not a life of regrets.
Remember that a little love goes a long way.
Life's treasures are people…together.
Do ordinary things in an extraordinary way.
Have health and hope and happiness.
Take time to wish upon a star.
And don't ever forget…how very special you are.

COLLIN MCCARTY

The Good Times

DAWN MILLER

from The Journal of Callie Wade

From now on, I am going to grab the good times with both arms. I am going to walk outside and feel the sun on my face and learn to laugh, really laugh again. Most of all, I'm going to take the love that comes my way and hold on to it for dear life. Sometimes we don't need new scenery, just new eyes.

Sunday Best

DORTHY CANFIELD FISHER
from A Harvest of Stories

One of the families in our town was very poor. The
father had died, the mother was sick, the five children
scratched along as best they could, with what help the
neighbors could give them. But they had to go without
things that you'd think were necessary.

They wore things that other people had given up because they were too ragged. Their mother, sitting up in bed, patched them as best she could, and the children wore them. When the oldest boy—he was a little fellow about fourteen years old—got a chance to go to work for a farmer over the mountain from our valley, he had nothing at all to wear but a very old shirt, some faded, much-patched blue denim coveralls, and his work shoes.

The farmer and his wife had never seen anybody in such poor working clothes. It did not occur to them that the new-hired boy had no others at all. Saturday when the farmer's wife went to the village to sell some eggs, she bought young David a pair of blue jeans, so stiff they could almost stand alone—you know how brand-new overalls look.

The next day at breakfast they said they were going to church, and would David like to go along? Yes, indeed he would! So they went off to their rooms to get into their

51

Sunday clothes. The farmer was dressed first, and sat down by the radio to get the time signals to set his watch. David walked in. His hair was combed slick with lots of water, his work shoes were blacked, his face was clean as a china plate. And he had on those stiff, new blue jeans, looking as though they were made out of blue stovepipe.

The farmer opened his mouth to say, "We're almost ready to start. You'll be late if you don't get dressed for church," when he saw David's face. It was shining. He looked down at the blue jeans with a smile; he ran his hand lovingly over their stiff newness, and said ardently to the farmer, "Land! I'm so much obliged to you folks for getting me these new clothes in time to go to church in them."

The farmer had to blow his nose real hard before he could say, "Wait a minute." He went to take off his own black suit and put on a pair of blue jeans. Then he and David walked into church together, sat in the same pew, and sang out of the same hymnbook.

May I softly walk and wisely speak
Lest I harm the strong or wound the weak;
For all those wounds I yet must feel,
And bathe in love until they heal.
Why should I carelessly offend
Since many of life's joys depend
On gentle words and peaceful ways;
Which spread such brightness o'er our days.

SHAKER POEM

Faith is a grand cathedral, with divinely pictured windows. Standing without, you can see no glory, nor can imagine any, but standing within every ray of light reveals a harmony of unspeakable splendors.

NATHANIEL HAWTHORNE

Faith and Doubt

AUTHOR UNKNOWN

Doubt sees the obstacles,

Faith sees the way;

Doubt sees the blackest night,

Faith sees the day;

Doubt dreads to take a step,

Faith soars on high;

Doubt questions, "Who believes?"

Faith answers, "I."

A Gift To Remember

CORRIE FRANZ COWART

Sometimes we find threads of life that bind generation to generation. Sometimes there are symbols that make family history alive in the present. When I sit down to play my grandfather's piano I feel this thrill. I hear him playing evening lullabies to my mother, passionate Beethoven for my grandmother, and playful jigs for me to dance to. Grandfather Lester's piano is a symbol of abiding love.

The son of a small-town preacher, Lester was not born into great worldly wealth. Rather than money, he received a virtuous upbringing in which he learned the values of self-reliance and undying resolve, and found his joy in the creative aspects of life. Captivated by his love of music, Lester chopped cords of wood to earn piano lessons.

Music is... the rainbow of promise translated out of seeing into hearing.

L. M. CHILD

The Depression meant an end to my Grandpa's college education, as well as his musical pursuits. He was thirty when he married his sweetheart, Frances, and the two of them began to make the sweet domestic harmony of a little home and family.

Lester's interest in music never subsided. Whenever he could, he listened to and studied the great classical composers. He didn't, however, have much of an opportunity to practice his own talents. With many bills to be paid and the prospect of children on the way, purchasing a piano for himself just was not practical or realistic.

In 1942 he was drafted and sent to the European front lines. Every day, amid the horrors of war, Lester found time to write to his dearest Frances. He longed to be home with her and the "little man," the name he gave their newborn son, in the "little mansion," the title he bestowed on their modest home. His cherished correspondence, carefully preserved, was read and reread, as every day Frances would anxiously await his next letter.

Lester sent all the money he could to support his young family, while Frances worked part time as a nurse to help make ends meet. Scrimping and saving, she lived on the bare necessities, praying continually for her husband's safety.

Then one day in March 1946, with the war over and Europe finally secured, Lester returned to his family in the "little mansion." To his surprise a gift of love awaited him. All the checks he had sent to feed his small family had been carefully saved to buy a gift to feed his soul. My

Grandmother, forgoing comfort for herself, had saved nearly every penny to buy a piano for her beloved husband. It was just a small spinet, but to Lester it could not look or sound better than the world's finest concert grand.

Though Grandpa Lester and Grandma Frances have passed from this earth, every note from this instrument sings of my grandparents' love for one another and their love for me still. It is music that connects across seas, through generations and beyond death.

The heart of the giver makes the gift dear and precious.

MARTIN LUTHER

Broken Dreams

LAURETTA P. BURNS

As children bring their broken toys

with tears for us to mend

I brought my broken dreams to God

because He is my friend.

But then, instead of leaving Him

in peace to work alone

I hung around and tried to help

with ways that were my own.

At last I snatched them back and cried,

"How can you be so slow?"

"My child," He said, "What could I do…

you never did let go."

Grandpa's Hands

CASANDRA LINDELL

Grandpa's hands were cracked and stained from years of farm work; his left thumb rounded backward, broken by a hammer years before. They were rough and scarred, but they carried warmth and strength.

Only three things mattered to Grandpa: his family, his land, and his God. He was a smart man when it came to practical things and common sense, but he wasn't one for "book learnin'." He never learned to read well. But when I stayed overnight at Grandpa's house I would listen to him and Grandma take turns reading the Bible. Its cover was as worn as the hands that held it. He stumbled over the awkward words, and many times he'd ask Grandma to look up the meaning of a word in the small dictionary they kept nearby. In recent months the dictionary had been misplaced.

Grandpa's hands held countless memories. They taught me to tie my own shoes when I was six years old. Once, a temperamental horse raised its back leg to kick my grandpa and I saw those firm, authoritative hands settle the hoof back to earth with one sharp slap and an abrupt command. I remember hands that scratched skin and snagged clothes when they tickled. Hands that gently cared for my grandmother at home until her death.

He lived and breathed his land. "You know," he once told me as we sat looking at the vineyard from the house, "sometimes people ask what my hobbies are." He nodded his head toward the vines as his eyes softened to look far away. He smiled. "That's my hobby, right out there. I never want to be anywhere else."

His hands were strong, rough, and warm until he died. My last fond memory came the night before his second open heart surgery. We walked through his yard toward the corral to feed the horses. He stopped short and laid one hand on my shoulder, then he pointed to a bush at the edge of the drive. A bird's nest—and I listened for the thousandth time about what a nuisance starlings are to farmers and how loud blue jays shriek early on a summer morning.

It is love that asks, that seeks, that knocks, that finds, and that is faithful to what it finds.

SAINT AUGUSTINE

Three days later, at the memorial service, I said good-bye to my grandfather by placing a new dictionary, along with his worn Bible, in hands that told so many stories. Inside the Bible were three grape leaves pressed between the pages.

Later that day, I stood at the edge of Grandpa's vineyard. Tears burned up my throat, spilled down my face, and left my insides hollow. Those strong, warm hands had lost their grip on this life but they had taken a stronger hold of the next. The hollow inside began to warm as I watched a handful of the rich soil sift through my own fingers. I brought the earth to my face and inhaled the smell of home. Grandpa never wanted to be anywhere else and in my heart I know that he never will be anywhere else— but home.

Vegetable Man

AUTHOR UNKNOWN

taken from Leadership Journal

An old man showed up at the back door of the house we were renting. Opening the door a few cautious inches, we saw his eyes were glassy and his furrowed face glistened with silver stubble. He clutched a wicker basket holding a few unappealing vegetables. He bid us good morning and offered his produce for sale. We were uneasy enough to make a quick purchase to alleviate both our pity and our fear.

To our chagrin, he returned the next week, introducing himself as Mr. Roth, the man who lived in the shack down the road. As our fears subsided, we got close enough to realize that it wasn't alcohol, but cataracts, that marbleized his eyes. On subsequent visits, he would shuffle in, wearing two mismatched right shoes, and pull out a harmonica. With glazed eyes set on a future glory, he'd puff out old gospel tunes between conversations about vegetables and religion.

On one visit, he exclaimed, "The Lord is so good! I came out of my shack this morning and found a bag full of shoes and clothing on my porch."

"That's wonderful, Mr. Roth," we said. "We're happy for you."

"You know what's even more wonderful?" he asked. "Just yesterday I met some people that could use them."

Life is made up, not of great sacrifices or duties, but of little things, in which smiles and kindness, and small obligations given habitually, are what preserve the heart and secure comfort.

SIR HUMPHRY DAVY

Others

HENRY WADSWORTH LONGFELLOW

Lord, help me live from day to day
In such a self-forgetful way,
That even when I kneel to pray,
My prayer may be for others.

Learn to Smile

EDGAR GUEST

The good Lord understood us when He taught us how to smile;
He knew we couldn't stand it to be solemn all the while;
He knew He'd have to shape us so that when our hearts were gay,
We could let our neighbors know it in a quick and easy way.

So He touched the lips of Adam and He touched the lips of Eve,
And He said: "Let these be solemn when your sorrows make you grieve,
But when all is well in Eden and your life seems worth the while,
Let your faces wear the glory and the sunshine of a smile.

"Teach the symbol to your children, pass it down through the years,
Though they know their share of sadness and shall weep their share of tears,
Through the ages men and women shall prove their faith in Me
By the smile upon their faces when their hearts are trouble-free."

The good Lord understood us when He sent us down to earth,
He knew our need for laughter and for happy signs of mirth;
He knew we couldn't stand it to be solemn all the while,
But must share our joy with others—so He taught us how to smile.

There is no duty we so much underrate as the duty of being happy. By being happy we sow anonymous benefits upon the world, which remain unknown even to ourselves, of when they are disclosed, surprise nobody so much as the benefactor.

ROBERT LOUIS STEVENSON

Whether the world is blue or rosy depends upon the kind of spectacles we wear. It's our glasses, not the world that needs attention.

AUTHOR UNKNOWN

A good life—and it's yours for the taking. You have but to put out your hand and all you've wished for will be in your grasp.

L. M. MONTGOMERY

The greater part of our happiness or misery depends on our dispositions, and not our circumstances. We carry the seeds of the one or the other about with us in our minds wherever we go.

MARTHA WASHINGTON

Daybreak

A wind came up out of the sea
And said, "O mists, make room for me,"

It hailed the ships, and cried, "Sail on,
Ye mariners, the night is gone."

It said unto the forest, "Shout!
Hang all your leafy banners out!"

It touched the wood-bird's folded wings,
And said, "O bird, awake and sing."

And o'er the farms, "O Chanticleer,
Your clarion blow; the day is near."

It whispered to the field of corn,
"Bow down, and hail the coming morn."

It shouted through the belfry-tower,
"Awake, O bell! Proclaim the hour."

HENRY WADSWORTH LONGFELLOW

Acknowledgments

A diligent search has been made to trace original ownership, and when necessary, permission to reprint has been obtained. If I have overlooked giving proper credit to anyone, please accept my apologies. Should any attribution be found to be incorrect, the publisher welcomes written documentation supporting correction for subsequent printings. For material not in the public domain, grateful acknowledgment is given to the publishers and individuals who have granted permission for use of their material.

Acknowledgments are listed by story title in the order they appear in the book. For permission to reprint any of the stories please request permission from the original source listed below.

"Now Playing: Sunrise over the Lake" by Ann Campshure, freelance writer, Menasha, WI. © 1999. Used by permission of the author.

"A Fresh Perspective" by Barbara Johnson. Taken from FRESH ELASTIC FOR STRETCHED-OUT MOMS by Barbara Johnson, © 1986. Used by permission of Fleming H. Revell, a division of Baker Book House Company.

"Yesterday and Tomorrow" by Robert J Burdette. Cited in MORE OF…THE BEST OF BITS AND PIECES, © 1998, The Economics Press, Inc., Fairfield, NJ 07004, 1-800-526-2554

"The Red Umbrella" retold by Tania Gray. © 1995. Used by permission. Idea adapted from notes in my object lesson file.

"Morning Song" by Ruth Bell Graham. Taken from LEGACY OF A PACK RAT by Ruth Bell Graham, © 1989 (Thomas Nelson Publishing, Inc., Nashville, TN). Used by permission of the author.